Calhouns Corner

Vol 1

D1553690

Follow on social media:

Instagram:
Calhouns_Corner

YouTube: Calhouns Corner

Mentions:

Krab N Tingz | NLFA | Sly Ent | LCPNterprise LLC.

I don't want to be Everything to Everybody...that leaves

Nothing for me!!!

During our time on this earth, we will constantly be put in situations where we have to extend ourselves to others. This can be in many forms, but ultimately its draining. Learn how to put yourself first. That may hurt some people around you but it's necessary to preserve your own mental health. Always save something for yourself.

If you fall, then crawl...but never, I repeat never stop **moving forward!!!** ♥

$\mathscr{K}$eep moving, just like those military days. The world doesn't care how bad you have been beaten up; it will continue to beat you. The way to overcoming its brutal attack is to show no pain, no fear and show all of your determination. The ending to a journey is only when the passion in your heart ceases to exist.

I'm proud of your progress...We still have work to do keep going #Strong

Sometimes we like to sit back and admire all the hard work and effort we have put into our lives. It's amazing at times how much we can really accomplish once we become discipline and focused on a goal. Stop, don't get to mesmerized, remember there is always work to be done. Being the best version of yourself is an everyday building process.

You damn right I like the life

I live!!!

*Y*ou only have one life. We don't get to choose it, but we do get to live it. If and when you get to live the individual freedoms of your own life, don't forget to enjoy the experience.

Speak it, Write it down, Pray over it, Focus positive energy towards it, Have FAITH in it, then Operate in it...Watch the success!! ♥

$\mathcal{T}$o manifest what you want, you have to keep your goals at the forefront of your life.

Your tomorrow could be

TODAY!!!

Why wait to complete your dreams. How many more rest days and not living your best life days are your willing to endure. Stop waiting for tomorrow, do it today. Your future self will thank you.

Stop hoarding information, pass it along to strengthen **later generations!**

$\mathcal{P}$ass information along while you can still. Humanity is smart enough to figure it out without you eventually but, we will figure it out faster if you help the process along by divulging knowledgeable information. Help the future stop hindering.

You are not the first person to go thru the situation you are in...gather yourself and

Overcome!!!

♥

Self-explanatory, you would like to think. You are 100% not the only person to ever experience hard times. Stop with the self-pity, look yourself in the mirror and remember who you are.

If you're not ready to be uncomfortable, then you not ready to be GREAT!!!

The normal way of living has never made a great leader. Being in situations that are unfamiliar, high stress, seemingly impossible and border line crazy is what made GREAT people who they are. Do not confuse GREAT with Rich.

It was written, allow the
story to unfold #patience

*A*ll the blessings your heart desires are already written in your story of life. Continue being an awesome person, and what is for you will manifest. Nobody can take away what is meant for you.

The most important and precious things you can get from a Man 👑 or a Woman 👑 is their LOVE 🤍 AND TIME 🕰️...FACTS!!! 💯

🤍

$\mathscr{W}$ hen you receive Love and Time from someone, treat it with care. Respect the fact people are not obligated to give you neither of the two. So, if and when you receive it, respect it.

You may not know it now, it **may take time for it to** manifest, but believe in the fact that you have a purpose **to be awesome in this**

lifetime!!!

♥

$\mathcal{Y}$ou will be awesome

during this lifetime.

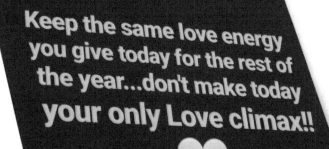

Keep the same love energy you give today for the rest of the year...don't make today **your only Love climax!!**

Put in the effort to treat the ones you love special every day. Love is unconditional...use it often!

Focus on building your brand...EVERYDAY the world should see your product and/or services. Become **more VISUAL!!!** ♥

$\mathscr{I}$f your product is not seen every day, then your product is not seen at all. Being consistent with your products marketing is key to gaining an audience. The audience is key to your income. Hold the keys then you hold the success.

*A*lways keep your foot on the gas, whatever your goal is. Keep at it, keep training, keep learning, keep grinding, keep elevating, it will I say again, it will pay off.

How do you find real genuine help in a selfish world? 🤔
🤍

$\mathcal{E}$verybody isn't for your best interest. Be aware of those who always look for something in return. The key to helping is to relieve stress and pain, and not to hold it over their heads. We all require help at some point but all help is not good help.

Nothing "NEW" can be gained by doing the same "OLD" things!!! ♥

*D*rop those old habits and train yourself to gain new habits. You don't have to necessarily change everything but sometimes upgrading processes is just as good as changing them. Think outside the box venture into the unknown and experience a NEW way of life.

Keep the same passion you had in the beginning!!! ♥

When the idea hit you, the fire burned extremely hot. Now that things are slowing down, you are not giving the same energy to your goal now. Remember why you started in the first place, channel that energy and get back to it!

$\mathscr{I}$f you know better than do better. Choosing to be a part of the chaos makes you apart of the problem...Be Better!

There is an audience for
EVERYBODY!!!
♥

*N*o matter what you do, no matter what your passion, no matter what your skills, no matter what your weird traits are, no matter what you like...There is an audience for everybody. So go start whatever you were thinking about starting, your audience is waiting.

Don't believe me, just

watch!!!

♥

The section for all the doubters is in the front. They need a clear view of your success.

Nobody in this world can stop you from your success. Be intentional with your goals and proactive with your actions.

Learn to have more control
of your Emotions!!!

Not being able to control your owns emotions can lead to someone else controlling them for you. This takes discipline and awareness to execute properly.

You have to Learn before
you Teach!!!
♥

*N*obody came into this world with all the answers. To successfully educate, you must obtain knowledge.

Something new is not always something better!!! ♥

Stop wasting your time trying to upgrade everything in your life. Some things only require cleaning, some things require shining and some things require a little bit of fixing up. When it's all said and done a little effort can revive what use to be old.

Confidence is key...Show the world your strength!!! ♥

The way you carry yourself is how the world will react to you. Stand talk, speak clearly and most importantly be sure of yourself.

Pay attention to the Leaches

$\mathcal{T}$hese individuals are always looking to take take take. Its ok to help but don't be a fooled by those that are scheming on you. The moment you can't provide they will detach.

Truth moment: I want YOU to succeed!!! #Truth ♡

$\mathcal{E}$verybody doesn't want you to enjoy success. Your success threatens them. There is enough space for us all to flourish and I'm routing for your success.

Enjoy the ride, you deserve
every blessing!!!
♥

When your blessing come in, enjoy them. Don't feel bad because those around you are not experiencing your level up. Block all the outside noise and enjoy what has been bestowed upon you.

Everyday is a brand new chance...If your Willing!!!

$\mathcal{A}$t the end of the day nobody can make you do anything...ijs.

Build your future with
Purpose ❤

When you know what you want, be specific in how you move and operate. Don't waste time with things that are not directly associated with where you are trying to go.

Do it yourself, the reward will be much more gratifying!!! 🤍

*T*he sweat equity that you produce to gain something makes it that much better to appreciate. Be apart of your own process, the satisfaction is unmatched.

Turn your Grind into a well
Oiled Machine
♥

In the beginning things will be a grind. It will take time to get operations flowing but once they do beware of the smooth sailings.

Take back Control of your LIFE!!! ♥

$\mathscr{T}$he time is now to be in control of who you are. We all fall down, but the key is to not stay down. Get up and reclaim your time.

Be a Blessing & recieve a
Blessing today!
♥

$\mathscr{I}$ believe the energy of the world returns what you put out into it. Blessing other people is our calling, and it will return back to you.

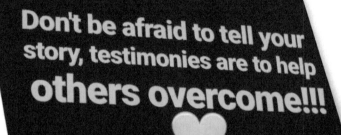

Don't be afraid to tell your story, testimonies are to help **others overcome!!!**

The road map to success
is hearing others speak on
how they made it. There
story will not fix yours but
it will help you navigate
because you now how
information that can assist
you.

We gon start this week off

Right!!!

♥

$\mathscr{I}$t's not about the day, hour or minute. Its about the now and how you have already spoken positive affirmation into your days ahead. Enjoy your week.

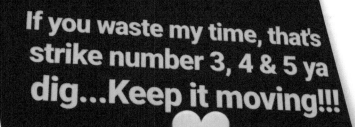

The most precious thing a human has in their life is time. We don't know how much we have until there is no more left. So why waste your time with people who don't respect yours. Don't waste your time.

Take a break from the norm...Shake it up!!! ♥

$\mathcal{I}$f life seems regular, its time to spice up your daily. Step outside of your comfort zone and do something new, exciting and exuberating. We are not built to be normal, let that sink in.

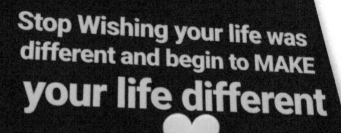

At what point in time will you realize that your life is in your control... Control it!

The process begins when you are ready...what you **waiting on?** ♥

$\mathscr{N}$obody is going to get the ball rolling for you. If you have a vision, start the work or it will perish from your mind.

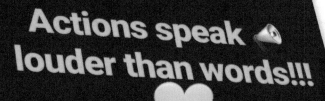

*O*ldie but goody, need I

say anything else.

Focus on your ENERGY, what you put out will return to you

Good & Bad
♥

Good and Bad energy returns back to the user. What type of energy do you produce and better yet what type of energy do you send forth into the world?

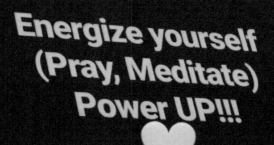

$\mathcal{I}$ challenge you to self-heal on a spiritual level. When you intentionally begin to elevate your mind body and soul, it's a guarantee you will be energized.

You are capable to be
GREAT at ANY level of your

life!!! ♥

Greatness can come at a young age or it can come at an old age. The last time I checked we don't have a timeline of when and how we spring into our greatness realm. Greatness can come at any point in your life, just be ready to answer the call.

Travel more...it will change your Prespective on Life!
#SeeTheWorld

$\mathcal{I}$f you haven't traveled to another country, you have deprived your own self of becoming a well-rounded person. The world is beautiful, I dare you to go see it.

How will you Utilize or Waste your time today? It's your

choice!!!

♥

We all have a choice...So what are you choosing to do with your time today?

Who really wants it...let me ask again because ya'll playing...WHO REALLY WANTS IT!!! ♥

People talk a lot about what they want but are not willing to put in the work to go get what they want. That makes no sense...smh

A genuine Goodmorning with a Smile 😀 can change a **vibe immediately #GoodMorning** 🤍

The vibe is easily manipulated and it starts with the introduction of feelings and moods. Be the first to introduce a vibe, smile to control the mood in your area.

I can feel the elevation of SUCCESS in the Air ♥

I feel it every day because I know I AM successful. How could you not feel it in the Air, its all around you...Success that is.

Have no regrets, own your

Journey

♥

*R*egardless of how your life turns out...OWN every minute of it!!!

Your dedication will be
matched with the right level
of success!!!
♥

$\mathcal{W}$hat you put out is what you are going to get back. So, if you're sitting there doing nothing...What you expecting to receive?

*T*hank you for taking the time out to receive some personal messages from me. I know the grammar and punctuations used were not all correct, but my intentions are for the information to be understood. I hope I accomplished my goal to give Confirmation, Inspiration & Motivation. Be blessed and in the meantime B E Z Breezy Yung Fly & Sexy.

*L*ucky *C*alhoun

Made in the USA
Columbia, SC
26 September 2021